# G You Didn't See *THAT* Coming...

## A brand new collection of strips

www.capesnbabes.com

**Written & illustrated
by Chris Flick**

**www.capesnbabes.com**
**www.csfgraphics.com**

## Credits and other stuff...

Written and drawn by Chris Flick
Book cover and design by Chris Flick

**Sketch Page...**

# ED REALLY DREADED THE DAYS WHEN THE SILVER SURFER NEEDED SOME QUICK CASH...

For a short time, I wanted to try my hand at styling my Capes & Babes characters more in the style of something like Peanuts and Charlie Brown. So I came up with the following strips and called them...

# CAPES & BABIES

**Sharping On Age...**

## New Kid On The Block...

## What Big Braces You Have...

**And Now You Know...**

OH MAN! I REALLY HATE IT WHEN YA GET TO DA BOTTOM OF A SLURPEE AN' ALL YER SUCKIN' IS NOTHIN' BUT _AIR_!

I KNOW _EXACTLY_ WHAT YOU MEAN!

UH... I THINK OUR SITUATIONS ARE JUST A _LITTLE_ BIT DIFFERENT...

OH, _REALLY?_ AND WHY DO YOU SAY _THAT,_ ROY?!!

SLURP!

UH...

I'M SIPPING OUT OF A _CUP_!

WAIT! LET ME GUESS...YOU NEVER TOLD HER I'M ANEMIC, RIGHT?

**Strict Rules...**

I CAN'T BELIEVE VAMPIRES HAVE SUCH A STRICT DIET, RONI!

OH, I KNOW!

SO, WHAT ABOUT _THAT_ GUY?

OH NO! HE'D BE THE WORST!

LIKE I SAID BEFORE...

I'M NOT ALLOWED TO EAT _ANY_ FAST FOOD!

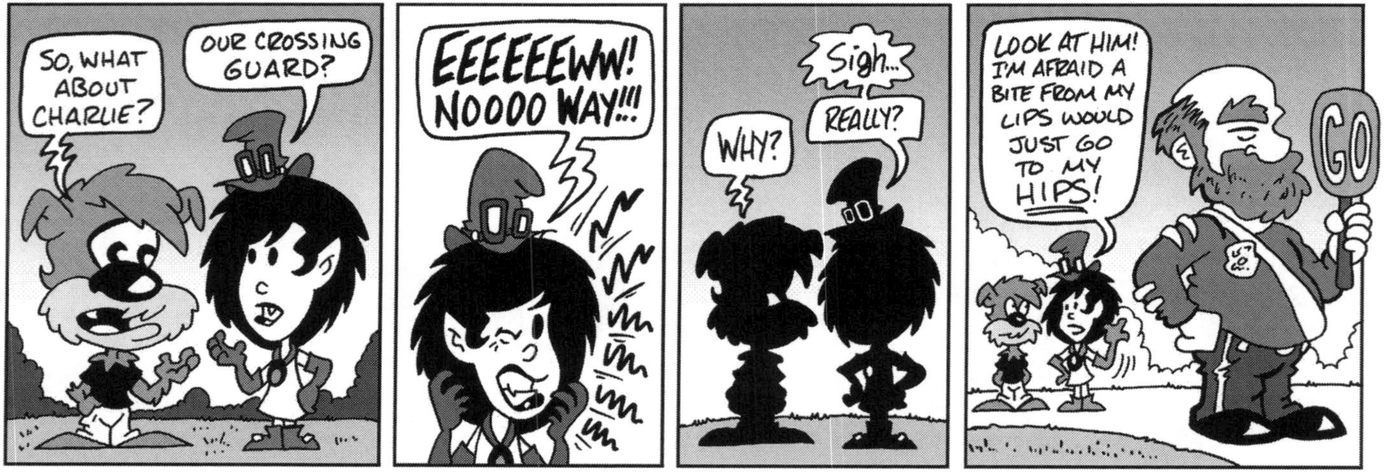
SO, WHAT ABOUT CHARLIE?
OUR CROSSING GUARD?
EEEEEEEWW! NOOOO WAY!!!
WHY?
Sigh...
REALLY?
LOOK AT HIM! I'M AFRAID A BITE FROM MY LIPS WOULD JUST GO TO MY HIPS!
GO

*Luck of the Wolf...*

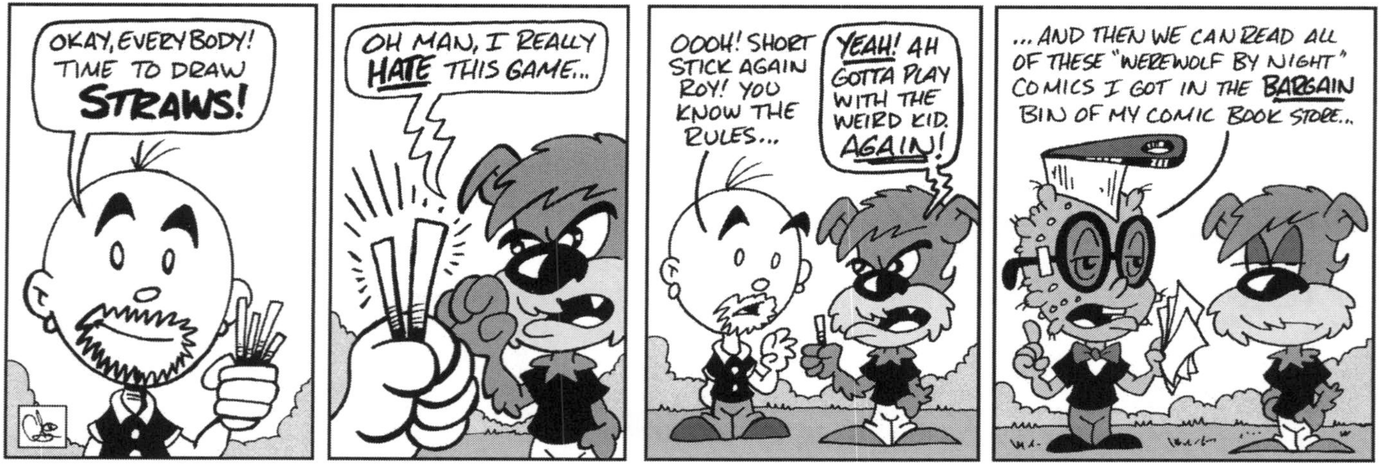
OKAY, EVERYBODY! TIME TO DRAW STRAWS!
OH MAN, I REALLY HATE THIS GAME...
OOOH! SHORT STICK AGAIN ROY! YOU KNOW THE RULES...
YEAH! AH GOTTA PLAY WITH THE WEIRD KID. AGAIN!
...AND THEN WE CAN READ ALL OF THESE "WEREWOLF BY NIGHT" COMICS I GOT IN THE BARGAIN BIN OF MY COMIC BOOK STORE...

**The Knoplauf Special...**

**Hospital Adventures...**

**Higher Mind...**

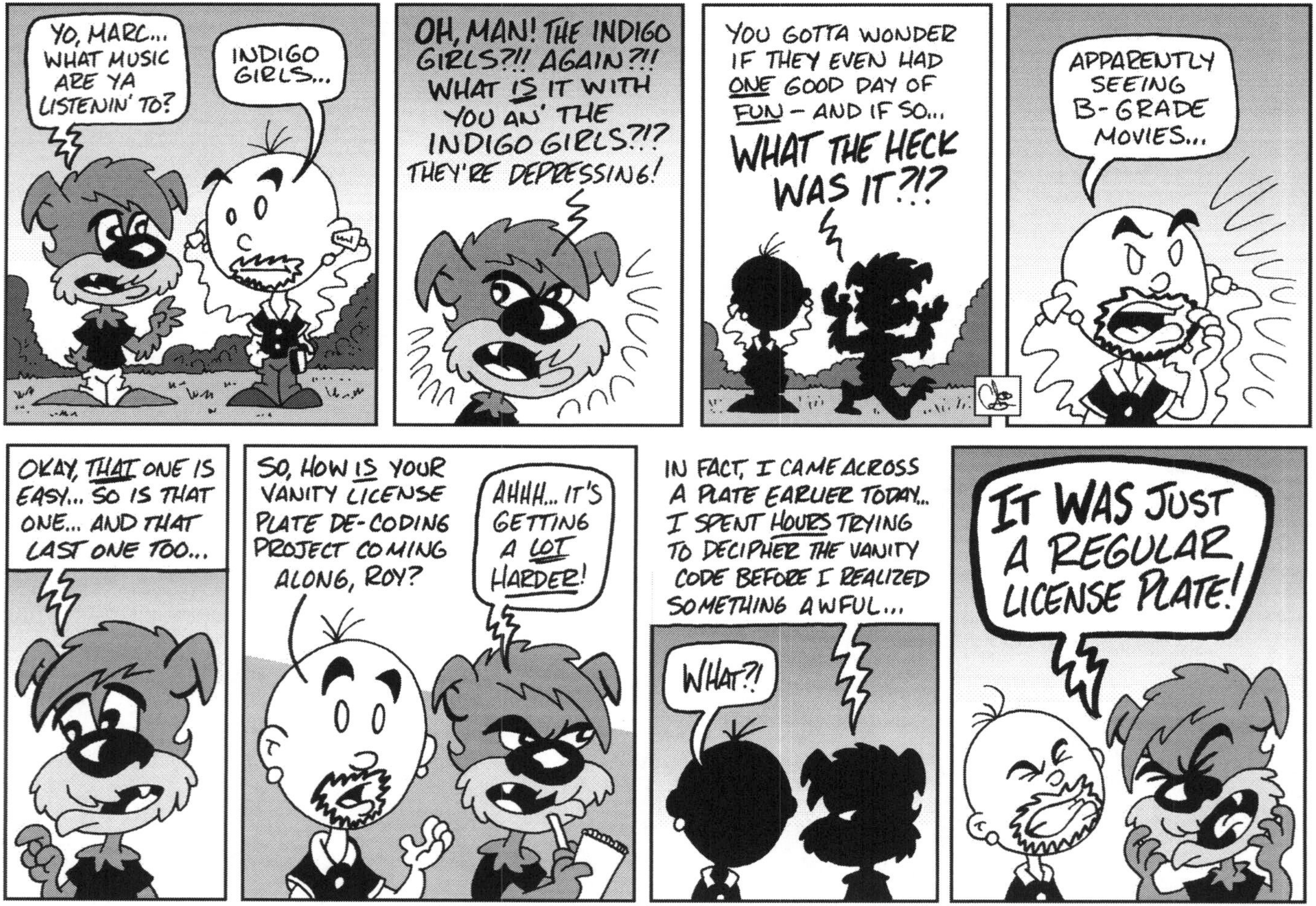
YO, MARC... WHAT MUSIC ARE YA LISTENIN' TO?
INDIGO GIRLS...
OH, MAN! THE INDIGO GIRLS?!! AGAIN?!! WHAT IS IT WITH YOU AN' THE INDIGO GIRLS?!? THEY'RE DEPRESSING!
YOU GOTTA WONDER IF THEY EVEN HAD ONE GOOD DAY OF FUN – AND IF SO... WHAT THE HECK WAS IT?!?
APPARENTLY SEEING B-GRADE MOVIES...
OKAY, THAT ONE IS EASY... SO IS THAT ONE... AND THAT LAST ONE TOO...
SO, HOW IS YOUR VANITY LICENSE PLATE DE-CODING PROJECT COMING ALONG, ROY?
AHHH... IT'S GETTING A LOT HARDER!
IN FACT, I CAME ACROSS A PLATE EARLIER TODAY... I SPENT HOURS TRYING TO DECIPHER THE VANITY CODE BEFORE I REALIZED SOMETHING AWFUL...
WHAT?!
IT WAS JUST A REGULAR LICENSE PLATE!

Gotta Cut Loose...

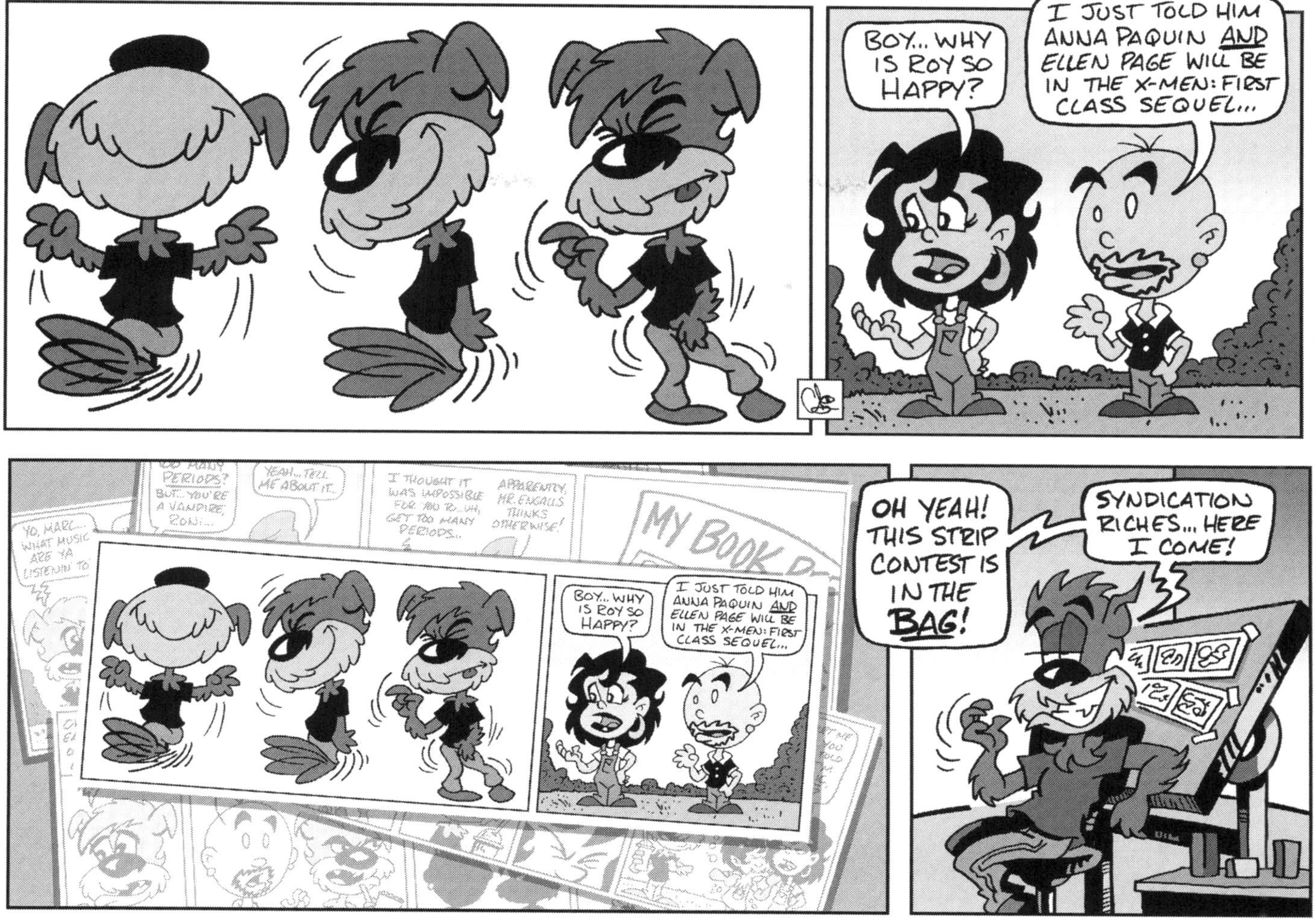

BOY... WHY IS ROY SO HAPPY?
I JUST TOLD HIM ANNA PAQUIN AND ELLEN PAGE WILL BE IN THE X-MEN: FIRST CLASS SEQUEL...
YEAH... TELL ME ABOUT IT.
I THOUGHT IT WAS IMPOSSIBLE FOR YOU TO... UH, GET TOO MANY PERIODS...
APPARENTLY, MR. ENGALLS THINKS OTHERWISE!
YO, MARC... WHAT MUSIC ARE YA LISTENIN' TO
BOY... WHY IS ROY SO HAPPY?
I JUST TOLD HIM ANNA PAQUIN AND ELLEN PAGE WILL BE IN THE X-MEN: FIRST CLASS SEQUEL...
OH YEAH! THIS STRIP CONTEST IS IN THE BAG!
SYNDICATION RICHES... HERE I COME!

"Field of Nightmares..."

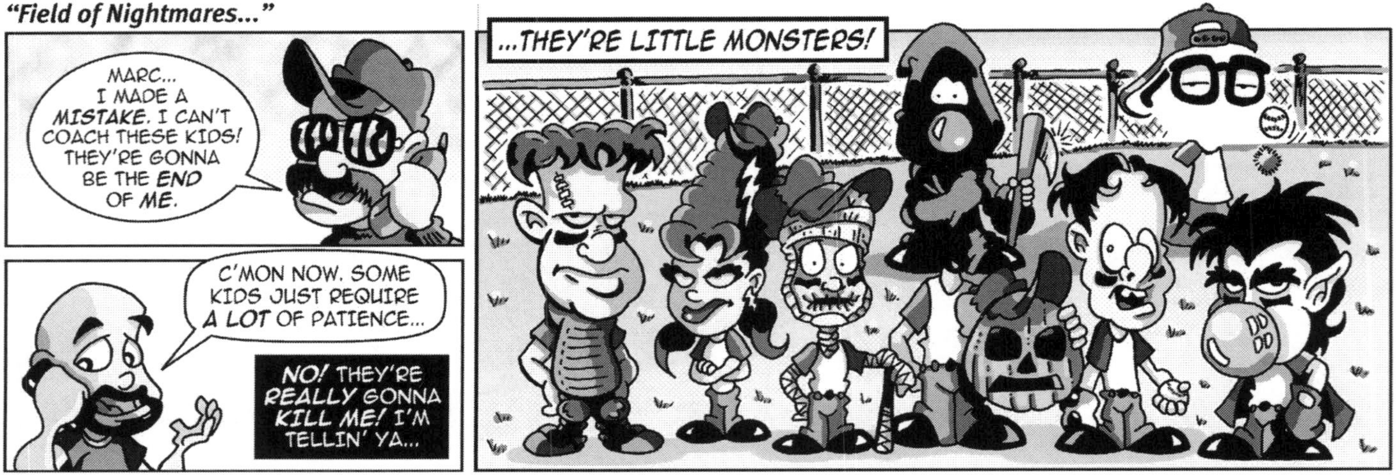
MARC... I MADE A MISTAKE. I CAN'T COACH THESE KIDS! THEY'RE GONNA BE THE END OF ME.
C'MON NOW. SOME KIDS JUST REQUIRE A LOT OF PATIENCE...
NO! THEY'RE REALLY GONNA KILL ME! I'M TELLIN' YA...
...THEY'RE LITTLE MONSTERS!

"Talk about the obvious..."

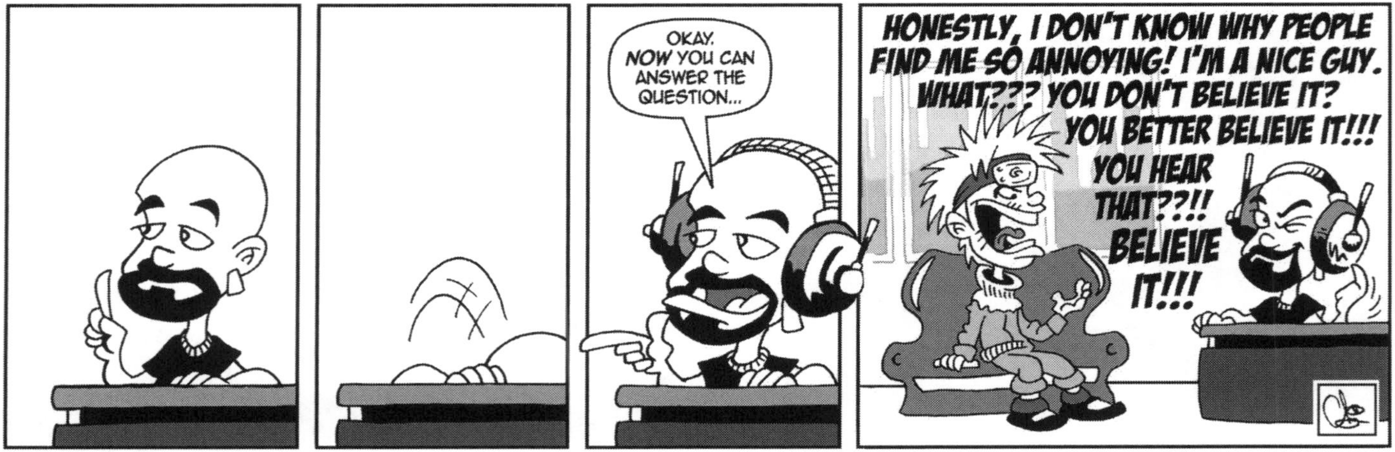
OKAY. NOW YOU CAN ANSWER THE QUESTION...
HONESTLY, I DON'T KNOW WHY PEOPLE FIND ME SO ANNOYING! I'M A NICE GUY. WHAT??? YOU DON'T BELIEVE IT? YOU BETTER BELIEVE IT!!! YOU HEAR THAT??!! BELIEVE IT!!!

## "Magically delicious..."

## I hate that song...

**Musical Duets...**

**Banana-nanna-fo-fanna...**

## "Master duplicator..."

FOLKS, YOU KNOW HIM AS THE BAD GUY WHO CAN *DUPLICATE ANYTHING* HE SEES. YES, TASKMASTER IS *IN THE HOUSE!!!*

SO, MR. MASTER... HOW ARE YOU?

HOW ARE YOU?

I'M FINE BUT LET'S TALK ABOUT *YOU.*

I'M FINE BUT LET'S TALK ABOUT *YOU.*

HAHA! I GET IT.

HAHA! I GET IT.

OKAY. STOP!

OKAY, STOP!

ALRIGHT! THAT'S *ENOUGH.* ARE YOU GOING TO BE A *JERK* THIS WHOLE INTERVIEW?

ALRIGHT! THAT'S *ENOUGH.* ARE YOU GOING TO BE A *JERK* THIS WHOLE INTERVIEW?

YOU KNOW... IT'S CHILDISH BEHAVIOR *LIKE THIS* THAT PROBABLY KEEPS GOOD WRITERS AND ARTISTS FROM WANTING TO *WORK* WITH *YOU!*

## It's a Trapp...

SO *THIS* IS THE INFAMOUS VIDEO PODCAST I'VE HEARD *SO* MUCH ABOUT!

UH.... THANKS...

ADMIRAL ACKBAR... THANKS FOR BEING MY AFTER-COMIC CON GUEST. I'VE...HEE! ADMIRED YOU FOR A LONG TIME.

I HEARD YOU WERE KICKIN' IT UP *PRETTY HARD* AT THE AFTER-CON STAR WARS PARTY... CARE TO SHARE?

OH YEAH- A BUDDY FROM OVERSEAS FLEW IN FOR THE CON... WE HAD A BLAST! HE'S *HERE!* WANNA MEET HIM? HE'S PRETTY COOL. HE'S **A TRAPP!**

♫ A DOE A DEER A FEMALE DEEEER! ♫

CAPT. VON TRAPP?!!?

OH YEAH... WE HAD A KICK ASS COLLEGE BAND BACK IN THE DAY? MAYBE YOU HEARD OF US? THE TRAPP BAND???

**Two Hit Wonder...**

HI MARC. GLAD TO BE ON THE SHOW!

LOU BEGA! WOW!! I UNDERSTAND YOU & MARVEL ARE TEAMING UP FOR A LITTLE CROSS-PROMOTION.

THAT'S RIGHT, MARC. I WROTE A NEW SONG FOR ONE OF MARVEL'S LATEST BOOKS & WITH ROY'S HELP, I'M GONNA SING IT RIGHT NOW!

HIT IT, ROY!!!

BOOP! BOP! BUMP.A.BUMP PA! BOOP! BOP! THUMP POP BUM PA DO!

I CALL THIS LITTLE DITY...

MARVEL ZOMBIES #5!

SNAP!

SMACK!!!

**Ultimate Answer...**

COL. FURY, IT'S SO COOL THAT YOU WERE ABLE TO STOP BY! BUT... BEFORE YOU GO, THERE'S ONE LAST QUESTION I HAVE ALWAYS WANTED TO ASK...

YES?

WELL, SIR, IF THE REGULAR MARVEL UNIVERSE HAS AN ULTIMATE NULLIFIER, WHAT DO YOU FOLKS IN THE ULTIMATE UNIVERSE CALL YOUR ULTIMATE NULLIFIER?

MARC... IT'S VERY SIMPLE, ACTUALLY...

WE CALL IT...

THE MOTHER [BLEEEEP!] NULLIFIER.

'NUFF [BLEEEP!] SAID...

**Bad hearing...**

When a construction worker's hearing goes bad...

**One nite only...**

***Should've been obvious...***

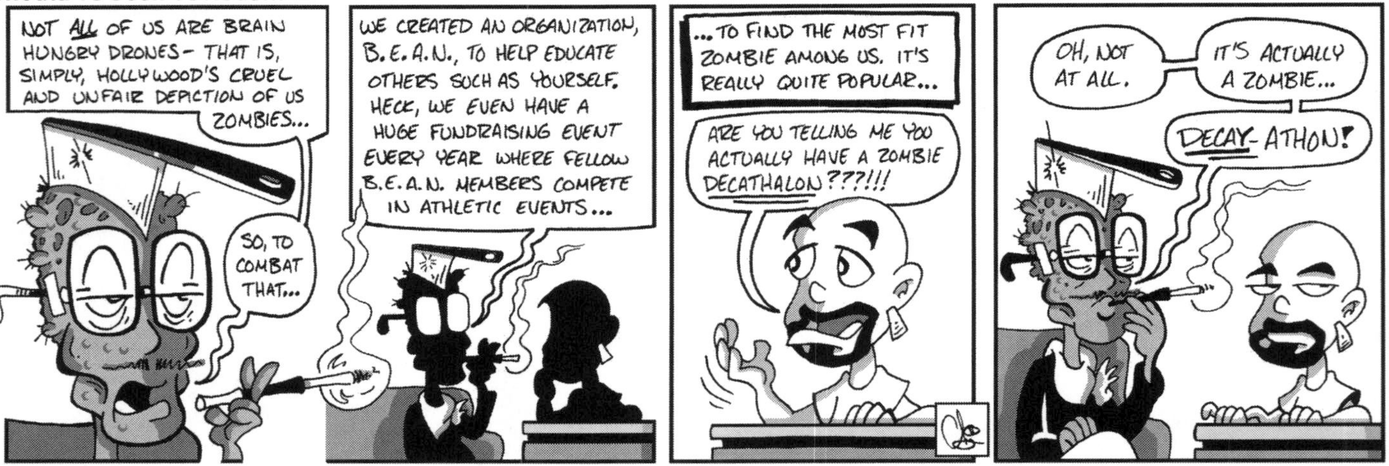
NOT ALL OF US ARE BRAIN HUNGRY DRONES– THAT IS, SIMPLY, HOLLYWOOD'S CRUEL AND UNFAIR DEPICTION OF US ZOMBIES...
SO, TO COMBAT THAT...
WE CREATED AN ORGANIZATION, B.E.A.N., TO HELP EDUCATE OTHERS SUCH AS YOURSELF. HECK, WE EVEN HAVE A HUGE FUNDRAISING EVENT EVERY YEAR WHERE FELLOW B.E.A.N. MEMBERS COMPETE IN ATHLETIC EVENTS...
...TO FIND THE MOST FIT ZOMBIE AMONG US. IT'S REALLY QUITE POPULAR...
ARE YOU TELLING ME YOU ACTUALLY HAVE A ZOMBIE DECATHALON???!!!
OH, NOT AT ALL.
IT'S ACTUALLY A ZOMBIE...
DECAY-ATHON!

***A day late & a head short...***

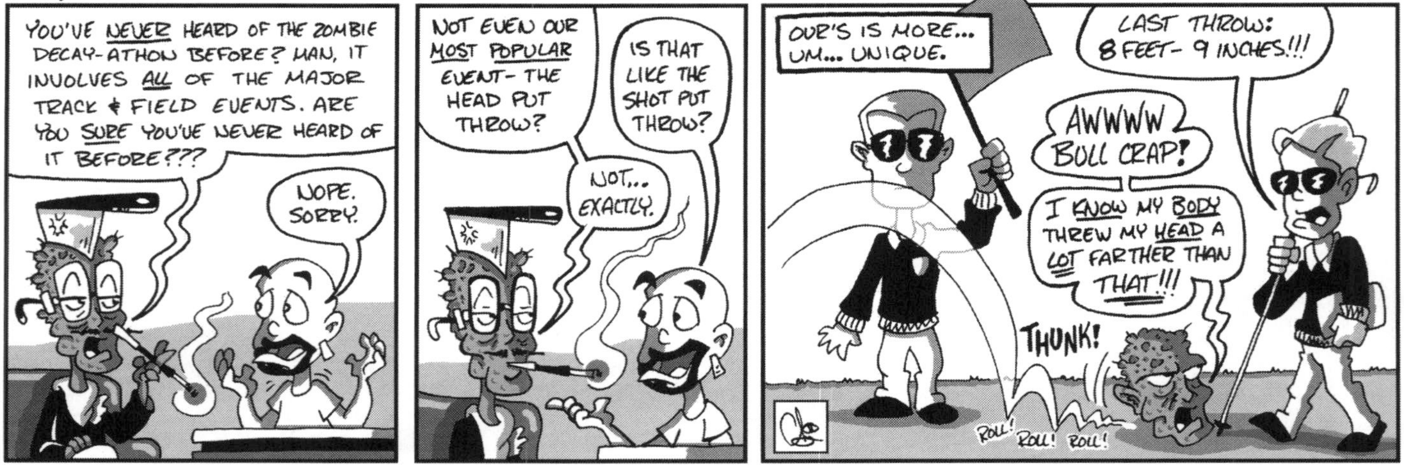
YOU'VE NEVER HEARD OF THE ZOMBIE DECAY-ATHON BEFORE? MAN, IT INVOLVES ALL OF THE MAJOR TRACK & FIELD EVENTS. ARE YOU SURE YOU'VE NEVER HEARD OF IT BEFORE???
NOPE. SORRY.
NOT EVEN OUR MOST POPULAR EVENT– THE HEAD PUT THROW?
IS THAT LIKE THE SHOT PUT THROW?
NOT... EXACTLY.
OUR'S IS MORE... UM... UNIQUE.
LAST THROW: 8 FEET– 9 INCHES!!!
AWWWW BULL CRAP!
I KNOW MY BODY THREW MY HEAD A LOT FARTHER THAN THAT!!!
THUNK!
ROLL! ROLL! ROLL!

## Fastest Zombie Alive...

## Endorsements...

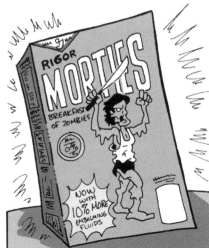

**Stick Training...**

**Yummy Twilight Star...**

**Bagel Bungle...**

AWWW, C'MON! IT'S TOTALLY NOT MY FAULT! I'M A WEREWOLF... I DON'T HAVE TO WORRY ABOUT WHAT I EAT. IS THAT SO WRONG?

THE BAGEL GUYS SCREWED UP...

I GOT HER CINNAMON & RAISIN BAGEL

WHILE SHE GOT MY GARLIC BAGEL...

THAT WAS MY SECOND GUESS...

**Zompathy...**

TRUST ME, I KNOW WHAT YOU'RE DEALING WITH, ROY. I USED TO KNOW A STARLET ZOMBIE WHO WOULD CALL ME ALL THE TIME.

SHE'D CALL ME & TALK ALL ABOUT WHICH ARM FELL OFF, HOW MANY BRAINS SHE ATE... I'M TELLING YOU, SHE COULD TALK ON THE PHONE FOREVER!

IN FACT, ONE COULD EVEN SAY SHE WAS THE EPITOME OF...

NO! DON'T SAY IT! PLEASE!

...THE TALKING DEAD.

**A likely excuse...**

**A New Business...**

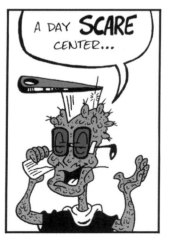

**Sith Lord Club...**

HEY, WHAT'S WITH THE HOOD & CAKE THERE, ROY?

MY SITH LORD CLUB MEETING IS TONIGHT.

WE'RE CELEBRATING "STAR WARS DAY" A FEW WEEKS EARLY AND IT WAS MY TURN TO BAKE OUR TRADITIONAL CAKE...

LIKE IT?

I DIDN'T KNOW YOU KNEW HOW TO BAKE! WHAT KIND OF CAKE DID YOU MAKE FOR YOUR SITH LORD CLUB?

EASY...

WE SITH LORDS EAT ONLY ONE KIND OF CAKE...

DARTH CHOCOLATE!

**Darth Planner...**

ROY, I KNOW YOU LOVE YOUR MEGABUY MEMBERSHIP BUT AREN'T YOU GOING A BIT OVER-BOARD?

NONSENSE. I'M THE PARTY PLANNER FOR MY SITH LORD CLUB "STAR WARS DAY"... WE'RE GONNA NEED 5 GALLONS OF THIS FRENCH ONION DIP...

FRENCH ONION DIP 5 GAL.

BUT... YOU ONLY HAVE A FOUR GALLON CAPACITY MINI-FRIDGE! I TOLD YOU THAT BACK AT MEGABUY BUT DID YOU LISTEN? NOOOOOO!

FRENCH ONION DIP 5 GAL.

DON'T MAKE ME FORCE CHOKE YOU AGAIN...

**Bad Date...**

**Panel 1:**
WAIT! YOUR SITH LORD CLUB CELEBRATES THE ANNIVERSARY OF STAR WARS ON MAY FOURTH?

DUDE!

YEAH... SO?

**Panel 2:**
STAR WARS OPENED ON MAY 25TH, 1977.!!! YOU GUYS HAVE BEEN CELEBRATING AN EVENT THREE WEEKS EARLY EVERY. SINGLE. YEAR.

**Panel 3:**
WHAT?! THAT'S IMPOSSIBLE! WE SITH LORDS DON'T MAKE MISTA—

GOOGLE SAYS: STAR WARS OPENS ON MAY 25, 1977 AND... THE SITH LORD CLUB IS FULL OF IDIOTS.

**Panel 4:**
DON'T MAKE ME FORCE CHOKE YOU...

**Bredi Special...**

**Panel 1:**
YOU'RE GOIN' TO BARRY'S BAKERY, AREN'T YA?

YEAH.

SO?

**Panel 2:**
LOOK, BARRY'S A GREAT BAKER BUT SOMEONE SHOULD TELL HIM THAT HIS OBSESSION WITH STAR WARS IS REALLY STARTIN' TA AFFECT HIS BUSINESS...

**Panel 3:**
BARRY'S BAKERY AND DELI SHOP

OPEN

WHY DO YOU SAY THAT?

**Panel 4:**
OOOOH... IT'S JUST A HUNCH...

TODAY'S BREDI SPECIAL: WHEAT OR WHITE, THERE IS NO RYE!

## Joining The Club...

YOU SHOULD LISTEN TO YOUR BROTHER. IT'S BAD ENOUGH I HAVE TO ALWAYS DEAL WITH JACOB & BELLA... OH LORD... HERE COMES YOUR BOYFRIEND.

HEY, GUYS...

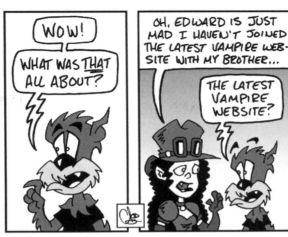

WOW! WHAT WAS THAT ALL ABOUT?

OH, EDWARD IS JUST MAD I HAVEN'T JOINED THE LATEST VAMPIRE WEBSITE WITH MY BROTHER...

THE LATEST VAMPIRE WEBSITE?

YEAH... FANGBOOK.

## Li'l Loki...

IT REALLY WASN'T ALL THAT EASY GROWING UP IN ASGARD, MARC...

REALLY. IT WASN'T.

OK, LOKI! HERE'S YOUR CHANCE TO FINALLY BE THE BIG HERO!

THIS IS IT!!! YOUR TIME IS...

TRIP!

HEERE-AHH!!

STUPID OVER-SIZED HORNS...

BONK!

**Secret Stash...**

**Conscience Object...**

**Glass Houses...**

**Costume Confession...**

**My Little Obsession...**

**Clean Up...**

**Brackets - Brackets - Brackets...**

**Master Disaster...**

**Meme Spoiler...**

*AGENTS OF S.H.I.E.L.D.

**SEE? TOLD YA...

**The Department of Catch Phrases...**

**Prejudicial Treatment...**

**Secret Pact...**

**Condiment Caution...**

**Wednesday Special...**

*Celebrity Contestant...*

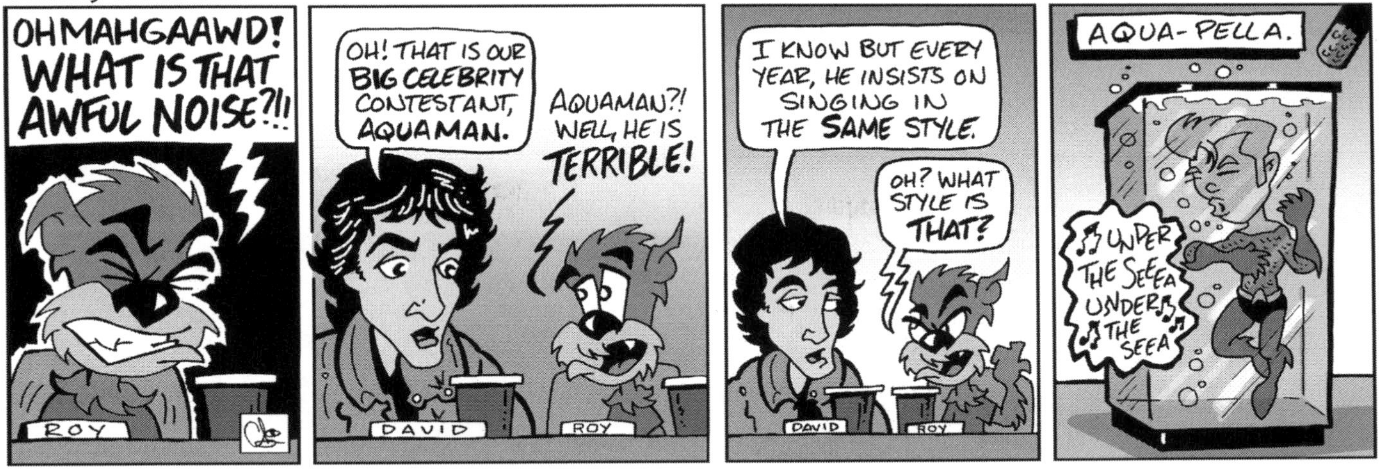
OHMAHGAAWD! WHAT IS THAT AWFUL NOISE?!!!
ROY
OH! THAT IS OUR BIG CELEBRITY CONTESTANT, AQUAMAN.
AQUAMAN?! WELL, HE IS TERRIBLE!
DAVID
ROY
I KNOW BUT EVERY YEAR, HE INSISTS ON SINGING IN THE SAME STYLE.
OH? WHAT STYLE IS THAT?
DAVID
ROY
AQUA-PELLA.
UNDER THE SEEEA UNDER THE SEEA

*Late...*

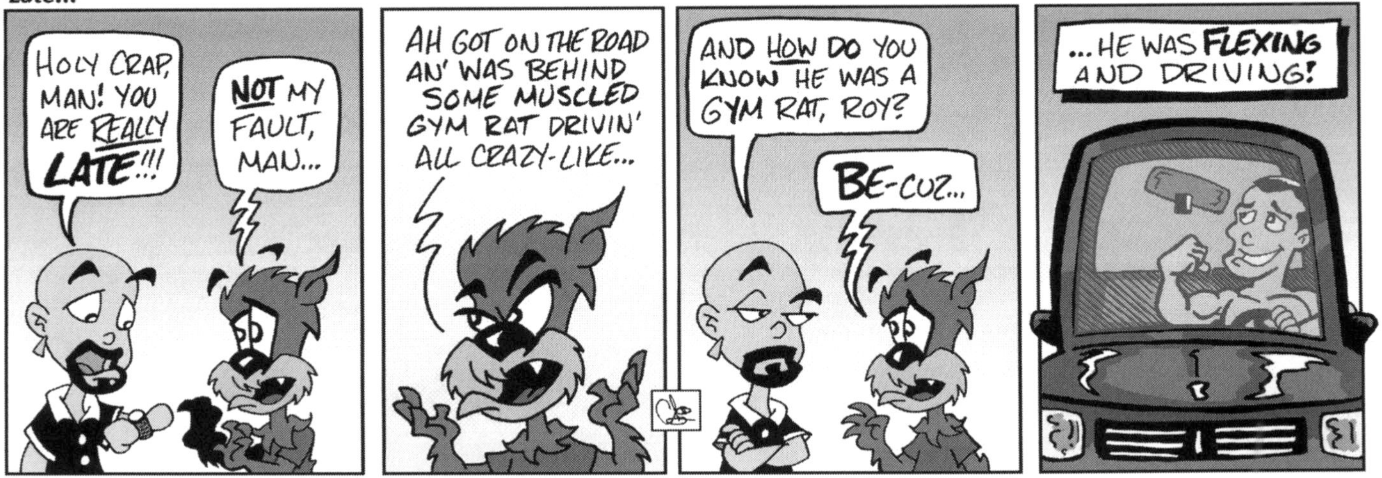
HOLY CRAP, MAN! YOU ARE REALLY LATE!!!
NOT MY FAULT, MAN...
AH GOT ON THE ROAD AN' WAS BEHIND SOME MUSCLED GYM RAT DRIVIN' ALL CRAZY-LIKE...
AND HOW DO YOU KNOW HE WAS A GYM RAT, ROY?
BE-CUZ...
...HE WAS FLEXING AND DRIVING!

# A very merry Christmas from Capes & Babes & Hans Gruber...

**Finding Roy...**

If you're wondering where Roy has been... after accidentally scaring a civilian at a bus stop, Roy was ordered to attend and take part in a Monster Sensitivity Training course.

The course is designed to teach monsters exactly why everyone views them as... well...um... Monsters...

MY WIFE & I WANTED TO SPEND A QUIET NIGHT NEEDLE WORKING BUT WE SCARED ALL THE STORE SHOPPERS...

I CAN'T EVEN STEP INSIDE MY FAVORITE GREEN & RED SWEATER SHOP ANY MORE...

... AND PEOPLE FREAKED WHEN I TRIED TO WATCH MY BELOVED RANGERS PLAY IN THE STANLEY CUP FINALS, MAN...

UH... CAN AH SIT SOME PLACE ELSE?

**Fear Itself...**

HOW CAN YOU BE A MONSTER SENSITIVITY COUNSELOR AN' BE PETRIFIED OF WEREWOLVES JUST BECAUSE YOU GOT BIT BY A REGULAR DOG ONCE?

I WASN'T ALWAYS AFRAID OF DOGS...

...BUT AFTER THAT, IT WAS CLEAR I WASN'T TAKING THE RIGHT PRECAUTIONS. I WAS TOO RELAXED WHEN I WOULD COME ACROSS A STRAY DOG...

OH MAN! AH'M *REALLY* SORRY! WHAT KIND O' DOG WAS IT? WAS IT A VICIOUS PIT BULL? A RABID GERMAN SHEPHARD? MAYBE AN OLD AND ABUSED DOBERMAN PINSCHER?

A BREED MUCH SCARIER.

A PUG.

**Con Selling...**

**Easter Egg Thingy...**

**The Last Straw...**

**"Sound advice..."**

**Marvel Universe Travel Tips: #145**

While visiting the Marvel Universe, never allow yourself to be talked into playing any kind of card game with the X-men, Gambit...

**Hall and Oates Karaoke...**

**"That's why he always losses..."**

## "Dee Plane! Dee Plane..."

### Plan of action...

**The Grand Finale...**

KEVIN SMITH... *WOW!* GOOD TO HAVE YOU HERE! OKAY, SO NOW THAT YOU'RE WRITING BATMAN, DOES THIS MEANS YOU'LL *ALSO* GO BACK *AND FINISH* THAT BULLSEYE AND DAREDEVIL STORY YOU *STARTED* – BUT *NEVER* FINISHED???

MARC, EVEN THOUGH *QUITE A BIT OF TIME* HAS PASSED SINCE I *ORIGINALLY* STARTED THAT STORY... I CAN TELL YOU I HAVE *FINALLY* WRITTEN THE *KICK-ASS* FINAL FIGHT BETWEEN DAREDEVIL AND BULLSEYE!

*DIE*, DAREDEVIL! *DIE* AS I THROW THIS OBJECT AT YOU!

DAMN MY ARTHRITIS!

*HA!* YOU'RE *PATHETIC!* ONCE I GET MY *WALKER* OVER TO YOU, YOU'RE GOING *DOWN*, BUSTER!

THUNK!

**Movie night...**

RONI MADE ME WATCH ONE OF HER FAVORITE MOVIES LAST NIGHT.

OH? WHAT WAS IT ABOUT?

IT WAS ABOUT THIS DUDE WHO HAD AN ABILITY TO SLIP INTO PEOPLE'S DREAMS SO HE COULD FIND OUT ALL OF THEIR SECRETS...

AAHH! INCEPTION! YEAH, THAT'S A GREAT MOVIE BUT IT'S BEEN OUT FOR A WHILE...

NOOO... THAT WASN'T IT...

WHAT WAS IT THEN?

UH... DREAM-SCAPE.

*DUDE!* I *HATE* THAT MOVIE!

**Golfing buddies...**

**Better than Avatar...**

Thanks for buying this book.

Here's hoping your entire family has enjoyed it.

And remember, if there's any references you don't get, there is always Google!

Made in the USA
Middletown, DE
12 August 2024

58576204R00024